First Kiss

How To Orchestrate An Ideal Opportunity For Intimate Kissing And Successfully Execute Flawless Kissing Technique

(The Most Exhilarating Experience For Adolescents)

Maurice Arias

After Gavin went home and showered, he returned to the back pasture. He and Satan rode the fence line for a couple of hours, looking for breaks. The only one he found was the one he'd made himself this morning. The pasture smelled like old smoke and rancid water, and everything was either black or covered in a fine coating of orange mist. He slid off Satan and walked around, not sure what he was looking for, but knowing that his sister was right; this fire didn't start itself. As he crunched through the charred brush, he thought about what they were up against with Tuck. The man had bought out the McGabes' ranch next door to them a little over a year ago. At first, they had all been friendly. Gavin and the ranch hands had even gone over a few times and helped Tuck with repairs on his barn and digging a deeper well. Then, all of a sudden, Tuck revealed his true colors.

Their new neighbor either found out or bought the land next door knowing there was a vacancy or a gap between surveyed tracts of land separating the main house of their ranch and where Tuck's land began. What that meant was that about four thousand acres of their land actually still belonged to the state of Texas due to a surveyor error. He filed an application with the Texas General Land office alleging a 3,992-acre vacancy. The lawsuit contended that the land was incorrectly surveyed and should be returned to the state.

The whole thing confused Kayla and Gavin at first. They couldn't figure out why this guy would care so much about land that wasn't his and wouldn't be his even if he won the lawsuit. If he won, the land would revert back to state land. Kayla had done a lot of research on the subject and her theory was, because of the way Texas law is written, a person who finds unclaimed state lands are compensated with a portion of the mineral output values in a vacant position. That finder's fee can wind up being worth millions, depending on the minerals. In addition to being entitled to the minerals' market value at the time of claim, the plaintiff's claim would eventually be dated to the original surveyor's field notes, which in the case of their family's land would be 1909.

If there were any minerals there, Gavin thought that sounded like a very reasonable theory. Their family had always been ranchers, and they were content with it. None of them had ever thought about whether or not there was another liquid or solid that ran through the land they loved so deeply, the land in their blood, that would make it so precious to anyone else. However, Kayla surmised that Tuck was counting on that. Gavin found it difficult to believe that the man, who appeared to have a sharp business sense, hadn't had more than a passing suspicion before proceeding with the action. Gavin understood very nothing about oil or any other resource that might be in the ground, even though he grew up in Texas. He was aware that finding it typically required significant funding and labor, so what would convince Tuck Stevenson that it was all worthwhile? He looked up as he considered the situation and noticed the sheriff's SUV approaching the trail in a dust cloud. Staying motionless, he observed Colt—the Cross River deputy, with whom Gavin had gone to kindergarten and high school—park and get out of his SUV.

"Colt, what brings you out?" I asked.

"You guys had a strange fire out here this morning, according to Wes Granger. You can only imagine my shock when I learned of it completely unawares. I figured I'd come up here and have a look for myself because when I stopped at the house, it appeared like Kayla had some guests.

Gavin gave a shrug. I suppose I mistook Kayla's earlier call for mine. That day has been one of those.

"Or you simply chose not to report it."

Or that, Gavin continued.

"Gavin, why not? Should Tuck Stevenson be frantically setting fires right now...

"We won't be able to prove he did anything, for starters, and every time you visit, there's more rumors and conjecture about what's happening in the community. As it is, I can hardly sell my horses. I don't want folks to assume we're constantly experiencing issues or my sales to completely stop. "We are not being driven off our land by Tuck Stevenson."

What is the status of the lawsuit? Do you believe you can defeat that?

Kayla feels that we can. I'm not sure. Why do you think Tuck Stevenson would give a ranch he doesn't appear to want a ton of money and then try to assist the state of Texas in taking my land?

"I believe there had to be a benefit for Tuck."

"I would say a great deal of stuff. That, in my opinion, is the secret to solving everything and preserving our land. Kayla and the attorney she is spoken with appear to believe that we can prevail in a court of law. I'm not really confident in it.

Does Kayla understand why?

With a narrowed gaze, Gavin told the deputy, "Nope, and she's never going to know, either." I have to leave for a meeting. You can search around all you want, but I doubt you'll find anything unless you have x-ray vision.

He felt his phone beep in his pocket as he turned to face Satan, who was waiting there. He saw his sister's number and the time when he pulled it out. Three minutes to fifteen. Even though he knew what lay next, he would much prefer wait and experience her wrath firsthand. After selecting ignore, he placed the phone back in his pocket.

"※'

Lucy Lancaster sipped tea in the comfortable country house recliner upholstered in plaid, listening to her brother's message from her anxious new customer.

Through gritted teeth, Kayla replied, "Gavin, it's three-fifteen." It has taken fifteen minutes for our guest to arrive. She arrived on schedule. How are you doing?

Lucy saw her take a deep breath and then put a beautiful smile on her face as she ended the call. "He ought to arrive any moment."

Lucy grinned back, wiping a curling lock of red hair off her forehead. "Stop worrying about it. I will remain in the city regardless if we are going to work together. It's not as though I need to rush there.

After taking a seat across from Lucy in the twin plaid chair, Kayla Walker ran her hand through her long, black hair. "Miss Lancaster."

Say please that I am Lucy.

Kayla smiled nervously. "Lucy." How much do you understand about Tuck's intentions here? Have you already handled a case similar to ours?

"No, I haven't defended anyone in a situation precisely like this. However, in my career, I have represented more than twenty-five clients, and my win percentage is ninety-eight percent. I only take on cases when I think there has been injustice or that someone is being mistreated by the government or, worse yet, large business. Tuck Stevenson may have been the impetus in your instance, but the fact remains that the Texas government enacted legislation of this kind for its own self-interest. They don't take into account that your family has been cultivating this land for — what was it you said? 84 years old? They wouldn't give a damn if your family was forced to relocate or faced financial devastation as a result of the plaintiff's victory. I find it infuriating that they are only concerned with making money.

Kayla's smile looked much more sincere and less nervous this time. "It infuriates me as well," she concurred.

"What is it that incites our rage?"

Lucy turned to face the voice. She seemed to be conscious of the man's unmistakable masculinity from the moment she looked at him, since his voice carried a distinctly masculine quality. He cast a glance at her with sharp hazel eyes, one of which had a shiner. The eyes did not appear hostile, but it was difficult to take your eyes off them. They appeared to be holding off on making a decision for the time being. With a start, Kayla glared at the man standing in the doorway.

She looked at Lucy after that. "Lucy Lancaster, this is Gavin Walker, my brother who is always late."

Lucy got to her feet, grinning, and extended her hand to Gavin, who hesitantly moved forward to accept it. She knew how his hard palm felt on her soft one, and how his skin smelled woodsy and manly. After shaking her hand, he released it.

Gazing about the space, he inquired, "Were you accompanied by the attorney or—?"

With an eyebrow lift, Lucy retorted, "I am the lawyer."

Gavin's expression revealed everything he was thinking. It was clear that she was not what he had anticipated. Would the fact that she was a woman give him any trouble? What century precisely was this cowboy living in?

Alternatively, she simply made it to the point of

It is true that when the first year of school started this year, ghosts and monsters attacked the Hogwarts train. Draco Malfoy should be thirteen years old, entering the third grade, as this body is 37 years old this year.

She shivered a little since the scene before her looked similar to the Hogwarts train.

This time, Naamah appears to be boarding the front of the train, and Lucius is adamant about getting Draco to go to school.

However, given her desire to attend Hogwarts, she is an outsider. She meticulously corrected a small mistake like a specter of the past, but then she started to get restless once more.

based She was, of course, because, in the previous year, Black broke out of prison while awaiting a variety of unfortunate circumstances, Lady Lawless was fossilized, and Deng Boi had multiple invitations to Hogwarts to take on a cat as a manager and bodyguard.

Miyeon found herself writhing her delicate face once more, and realized that this perverse woman's recollection often made her feel sad.

This pervert has far too much work to do. After graduating, she frequently enlisted Voldemort's assistance through Slytherin to join the magic department as an Auror and subsequently conduct additional research. reveal to her the name of Lucius the Death Eater, steadfastly uphold the values of love, and she quit after she became recognized as an authority on miraculous animals and published an excessive number of books, irrevocably This year, Deng Boi extended numerous invitations to Hogwarts to be the cat manager the night before the school began.

Don't you suppose your brain is still longer than a pig's based on what scientists don't do, which is to let people guarantee the spending? Miyeon was mad in the dark.

An actual person's fury tends to overestimate the tiny echo, making it impossible for her to see the supposed echo at all.

It had already been a hit back, a neck strike on the frigid face, by the time her senses returned.

"A hand reached out from the cloak, this pointed out a pale, gray light, thinner and more scaly, like something dead, immersed in rotten water again," she said, raising her head and taking a slow, deliberate glance at the spot where the frigid air had congregated. The other hand seemed to be empty. to a complex second. The other hand abruptly rolled up the folds of the black cloak, and the monster's cloak felt as though someone was peering at it. Then, whatever the thing was, the hooded cloth beneath it took a breath, slowed down, and trembled again, as if trying to draw in air from the surrounds and expel some outside air. objectOnce more, an odd and peculiar string of black characters struck her mind, one by one. She was like a wooden head, foolishly remaining motionless while scribbling down the initial synopsis for her own comprehension.

By the grace of God, you are truly manipulating me.

------oOo-----Give you a good person card (Chapter 4)

"How? I've heard that NaamahNaamah visits your home frequently; you must be quite acquainted with her; you shouldn't need to summon her midwife every day."

Draco was going to make fun of Lin for taking the train, thinking he was the messiah terrified of the ghost, but instead, they caught up with them and the three of them ran into problems with the new black magic defensive class. The feminine identity has changed as a result of the other explanation group.

Name He will come naturally to the impoverished family since Naamah is a very famous woman who loves her family and has no one who doesn't comprehend.

Don't let this chance to make fun of him slip by.

What irritates me the most is that the new teacher truly used this to ask whether he was so comfortable with the woman that he allowed her to bring her bags. Oh, another foolish Gryfindor; he looks like a small elf in a rage.

However, he secretly understood that he was powerless to openly disagree with the new instructor, so all he could do was detest the subterranean train that carried a little child everywhere in a suitcase. The second woman was a disaster because she didn't know where to go when she died too soon.

Does the guy look like a Slytherin?

Ignorance, obstinacy, conceit, and the delusion that I am winning my father over!

It's hilarious how his mother gave him away in such a classy, dignified, and well-known way. Her disposition is a hundred times superior than his, so how can a father ever appreciate her?

She conceals her age, of course, and is perverse enough to study magic. She believes she is a woman.

Is closeness a face?

Furthermore, what memory does she have? Can she carry her own bags and forget them in the higher train? Hurry and put your life in danger with Longbottom.

She secretly cursed the deviant woman, yet she glided phantomly toward him when he hurried to the altar.

Alright, that was fantastic," I say to Caleb as we exit the ping-pong area.

He smiles down at me. "I guess we made a good team."

I pause my stride and turn to face him, and he follows suit. Indeed. Who knew?

He laughs, "Maybe I should go find you whenever someone asks me to play beer pong." However, that doesn't sound humorous. He appears to be sincere.

Not that it bothers me in the least. As I mentioned, I had a great time. In fact, I'm kind of excited to work with him once more. What other party games can we play really well together, I wonder?

However, that calls for more time spent with Caleb. Do you really want that?

"As long as we keep winning, I'm all in," I assure him, ignoring that persistent query.

Caleb smiles. "Try to stay up with me, please."

Please. That was insignificant.

"Well, you two seem cozy," I said.

Oh no. What is Jenna's current desire?

I can't help but smile as I turn to see her bringing the two of us closer together.

"I was informed about your small game." Even though she is grinning, it is obvious that it is phony. "Happy you're enjoying yourself at my party."

"Well, Jenna, we can't follow you around like a puppy for the entire night."

She adds, gritting her teeth, "Nobody asked you to do that, Nelly," her smile wavering a little.

Hehe! She is growing weary of being polite. Sooner or later, she will stop the act. Most likely before this conversation is over.

"Well, Jen, is there anything you need?" As if to remind her of his existence, Caleb interrupts.

As if she'll never get over him.

I've always assumed that Caleb dumped her, not the other way around as she claimed to have told everyone. When they were together, she seemed to be more into him than he was into her. She gave her entire personality to becoming his girlfriend for a very long time.

It was pitiful and eerie in equal measure.

In all honesty, nobody knows why they broke up. She posted a selfie to Instagram a few months prior with the remark, "single and ready to mingle." She then posted indignant selfies and thirst traps over the following few weeks.

It took me a while to accept it.

And it's clear from looking at her now that she hasn't moved on. She still has a strong attraction to him. I'm curious as to whether she still thinks they will reconcile.

Oh no. Hopefully not.

Even though we've only been hanging out for a few hours, Caleb already seems like such a nicer person than she does. Really, what on earth did he see in her? Throughout their junior year, they dated. She had to be someone worthwhile to be a girlfriend for that amount of time.

However, he doesn't appear to be aware that she is a true jerk.

Then he must immediately open his eyes. since she isn't the appropriate girl for him.

Furthermore, who is? You?

Whoa. How in the world did that idea occur to me?

"Hello? Do you even have a microphone?

It takes me a minute to remember that Jenna is still conversing with me. After a few blinks, I inquire, "Uh, what were you saying?"

"Oh, what a miserable thing." Jenna looks across at Caleb. "While you were playing, did she hit her head or something else?"

"Jen," cautions Caleb.

How come? All I wanted to do was ask. I'm concerned for her. She looks back at me. Nelly, do you need to lie down? Here, we offer an abundance of rooms. Even spending the night is possible. She tries to grin at me, really, but all it does is seem eerie.

She cannot act any more kindly toward me than I do. It's always turned out to be a lie.

Alright. I can't afford to be careless with her. She still seems like she might be planning something for tonight.

"Jenna, that is really lovely." However, you shouldn't be concerned about me. I have plenty of self-control." I smile at her as sweetly as I can. However, based on Caleb's wince, it appears to be equally eerie as Jenna's.

That's awful to know we share that trait.

"Are you certain? Because you recall from your freshman year? During our field trip, you ended up passing out in front of others. That is not something we want to recur, is it? That was really embarrassing. To be honest, I had no idea how you accomplished anything that day. I would have immediately returned home if it had been me. However, you were adamant about completing the journey. You know, one of the things I find admirable about you is that?

And there it is. An attempt at degrading oneself.

Hehe! Well done on the attempt.First, I had food sickness and puked. Secondly, I believe, if my memory serves me well, that I wasn't the only person who puked in public. We were around twenty when we got poisoned. It so occurred that I was the first to experience the effects.

Indeed. I recall throwing up three times that day alone. Caleb gives a headshake. "That episode of food poisoning was horrible."

You were one of them, I see. Jenna seemed nearly distraught.

I suppress a smile. She desired to focus just on me. to make me look bad in front of Caleb, but it was a complete failure.

She is so dull.

I give Caleb a slight eyebrow raise as if to say, "See what I'm talking about?"

He sighs and gives a nod of his head. Alright. He has come out of denial. Just as he opens his lips to speak, I get bumped into.

I can then feel the icy liquid trickling down my front.

"Oh, I apologize so much!" Dana Clancy, a red Solo cup in her hand, gapes at my dress with a terrified expression.

Dana, my god. Why didn't you exercise caution? You've now damaged Nelly's dress. Jenna gives a dissatisfied, "click-y" sound to her friend.

However, I am aware of better. The obviousness of it is almost comical. Liquid spilling down a girl's dress is the most stereotypical thing ever.

It smells like beer, which is something I detest.

And is this Jenna's grand, evil scheme? To be thrown beer at by her friend?

Oh no. Horrible. So pathetic.It was an accident, I promise. I was completely unaware of her presence. Dana says, "I'm so sorry, Nelly," to me. She doesn't seem apologetic at all, though. Indeed, it appears that she is concealing a smile.

"Oh really?" I stutter.

She gives me a scowl. "What's the intended meaning of that?"

Caleb grabs my hand before I can respond, surprising not just me but also the two girls.

I quickly look up at him. How is he acting?

"Go ahead, please. He tells me, "Let's clean that up," appearing irate for some reason. Without saying anything further, he then takes me away from the girls.

"Where are you going, Caleb?" However, Jenna's whimpering voice is ignored.

Taking Out Nana Lily pushed a huge wheeled suitcase at her after giving her a roll of black bin liners.

"It should go without saying, but just to be sure: clothes, trash bags, and items that shouldn't be donated to a charity; items to keep in the suitcase."

"I got it," I tell her as I make my way down the hallway to the bedroom of Grandma and Grandpas.

"And Celia?"

Indeed?

"I'm only allowing one suitcase full of memories; we can't get too sentimental." Dad doesn't know who we are, and Mum is obsessive about mementos, so

Even though only one of my great-grandparents has passed away, I don't need to be reminded that we have lost both of them.

"I will be packing up my room next door if you need arbitration."

When Grandma's health began to deteriorate a few months ago, Nana moved back in with her parents. When I was a baby, Grandpa Joe was killed in a construction accident, and Nana Lily has lived alone ever since. Kind of wonderful, I thought, that she had company again.

I take a big breath and head inside the bedroom. For as long as I can remember, everything has always been the same. The room is dominated by the double bed, which is flanked by a dresser and a wingback chair by the window. As the dim light from the outside comes in, I flip the switch next to the door. Yes, strong light is a great way to drive out spirits.

I half close the door, exposing the built-in double wardrobe behind it. It fills the majority of the wall. Smoothly, the door glides on its rollers.

The side of Grandpa is empty. When Mum and Nana Lily realized that

Grandpa would not be leaving the hospital following his stroke, they cleared everything up. He was in the care facility with the majority of his possessions. They sent the remainder to thrift stores.

Mom was so distraught at packing up Grandpa's life that she vowed never to do it again. I had taken the day off work to assist Nana Lily in packing up her childhood house in preparation for moving into her new, bright, two-bedroom home near us.

I fall to the ground and rip off two bags containing shoes, one for the charity shop and the other for the rubbish. Grammy, she loved shoes. Her feet were very delicate, and she had left some beautiful, barely worn shoes behind. It was unfortunate that none of us could fit inside them.

For her, Grandpa had constructed a unique shoe rack in the wardrobe's base. I made my way through the square cubbyholes from right to left, pausing sometimes to take in the beauty of some of the shoes. Reaching into the darkness of the upper left corner, my fingertips found a cardboard box instead of shoes.

With both hands, I reached in and took it out, then I plopped back down on the floor, sitting cross-legged, with the old shoe box nestled in my lap. I dust off the top layer of dust before opening it. I anticipated discovering a cherished and unique pair of shoes within.

"Ah, Grams!" What is the purpose of this? I say, my gaze fixed on a picture resting atop a stack of papers.

The man she was kissing in the midst of what appeared to be V Day celebrations was obviously not Grandpa, but the woman was unmistakably a young Grammy. Yes, he had the same tight black corkscrew hair and brownish-black skin as Grandpa and wore an American Air Force uniform, but he must have been six feet tall.

Grammy was five feet four, and Grandpa was only an inch or two taller.

I carefully lifted the black and white picture to reveal a stack of letters hidden underneath that were tied with a ribbon. All of them had prominent postmarks from locations in England and were addressed to my great-grandmother. A cursory glance at them revealed that they are arranged in chronological order of postmark.

I set the box and the picture next to each other and take up the first envelope.

The school found it quite challenging to release her so early. She was not only had to come here to serve as a volunteer teacher, but she was also in difficulties right now and would soon be without a place to live.

It won't help to talk too much, so simply leave if you can.

Layla: [Please keep the phone free at all times; if you need anything, don't hesitate to get in touch with me. This lady will fly and beat everyone who dares to abuse you till he dies!]

..

Mrs. Eva invited Kate to supper.

Though she thought it wasn't a smart idea, Kate was a little hesitant to go.

You can handle the food problem yourself, she had earlier told Mrs. Eva, but Mrs. Eva continued calling to go out to eat.

Given that Mrs. Eva must pay for her food and does not like to eat it all day every day, Kate also considered bringing Mrs.

However, Mrs. Eva rejected it.

She explained that none of the food was purchased; her family farmed the chickens and ducks, and she didn't spend any money—she didn't even take any, naturally.

However, she no longer leaves the house because she is aware that Mrs. Eva is not the only person she has.

Mrs. Eva gave her a lengthy call.

"It's a waste if you don't eat the delicious dishes that she makes." "Hurry up and leave, the food will get cold later," Mrs. Eva gave her advice.

Kate continues to listen as Mrs. Eva speaks.

Yes, there was a second individual seated at the dining table.

Kate dared not to stare directly there; instead, she just ventured to cast a cursory glance that gave her eyes a general idea of what was there.

Kate, please have a seat. Kate was dragged to sit behind Mrs. Eva.

They set down the chopsticks and bowl in front of him.

Mrs. Eva grinned broadly with great happiness; this afternoon, her lips had never lowered.

"This is teacher Kate; I haven't had time to introduce myself yet."

"Andrew, this is your nephew."

Mrs. Eva said, "Kate is one year older than me, I have to call her sister," pausing when she was done talking and grinning.

Andrew laughed quietly before he could say anything more.

It was a rather disdainful tone.

For my part, I have no idea what shame is.

Are you not concerned that your life will be ruined because he called you that?

Glancing over at Mrs. Eva, Kate smiled grudgingly.

There was something unsettling about his aura that practically made people shudder. Kate was really uncomfortable and had no desire to eat.

"Come on, you guys are all chicken thighs." Mrs. Eva arranged the chicken thighs in a bowl big enough for two.

Recognizing her nephew's disposition, Mrs. Eva remained silent and continued to remind them to eat.

Even though she is getting older, her favorite thing to do is watch her kids enjoy the rice that she made. She feels so happy and comfortable when she eats well and in large quantities.

Kate found it difficult to swallow her dinner overall.

I experienced severe agony during meals. It was unknown to me what I was eating or how much. My hand was so rigid that it was grasping chopsticks.

At last, the meal was completed.

Mrs. Eva was called outside the door at this moment, and it appeared that she was in need of a loan.

After saying her goodbyes, Mrs. Eva got up and left right away.

Thus, Kate and Andrew are the only two individuals remaining.

Tell me if it's okay. "You live in my house and still force the old woman to serve you every day?" shoving his chopsticks aggressively.

The chopstick-dropping hand moved by her sight; the fingers were thin, the joints were clear, and the hand's hue was that of healthy barley.

My hands looked wonderful, and that was the first thing that sprang to me.

Tell me, are you deaf? It's obvious that this adolescent has a highly fiery temperament.

Kate set down her fork and lifted her head out of instinct.

Startled right away.

The young man had delicate facial features, vicious eyes, a dark, bottomless appearance, an insanely wild body, and unbridled wildness.

Totally unlike the haughty, tattooed scoundrel that Kate had in her mind.

In all honesty, Kate had never seen a man with such good looks in real life.

He must be considerably inferior even to the TV person standing next to him.

She responded, expressing disbelief for a brief while before declaring, "Tomorrow I will find another place to live and move out."

She was also unable to claim that she had to depart right away. She was not going to get upset no matter how hard he chased people away.

She couldn't find suffering on her own, and even if she left now, she wouldn't have anywhere to go.

Her lips were slightly pursed, and her eyes were clear and serious, as if she wanted to assure everyone that she was telling the truth.

She was truthful.

Andrew averted his gaze, gave a little reprimand, and felt his heart quicken in anticipation.

Oh no, I was wrong to assume he was a liar at first, but he appeared feeble, spoke politely, and was a teacher.

He got to his feet.

"Leave right away."

After finishing his sentence, he turned to face the door.

He walked outside to investigate what was going on since it sounded like he heard someone chatting to his grandmother.

Kate sighed with relief as she finally blinked.

I felt a little awkward for a little while.

What other options did she have? Are mats really necessary to be spread out in the office?

Andrew left very early in the morning.

Adam's father thrashed him and kept him inside the house for a day as soon as the young boy returned home. He slipped away early in the morning while his father was still asleep.

"Andrew, you mentioned we're back at home. What should we do now?"

"Go find something to do if not."

"Last time my dad said that the car repair shop was recruiting apprentices, I felt like I could try it out."

Andrew ignored it and focused on the future.

He turned to look at him after a while and remarked mockingly, "It looks like you've woken up from being beaten."

With a sheepish smile, Adam rubbed his head.

"That's not the case... For the most part, I felt after giving it some thought that my dad was right to chastise me—I can't carry on like this every day.

Adam wanted to speak with Trinh Phong about business, so he risked everything to slip away.

However, he found that Trinh Phong's ideas weren't present.

Adam couldn't help but keep gazing over as he was constantly looking ahead this early in the morning.

not able to see anything.

"Andrew, do you really want to send that teacher away?" Adam questioned, changing the topic as he recalled why Trinh Phong had returned this time.

"I've heard that the principle was forced to visit your home because she genuinely didn't have anywhere else to stay. She will actually have to eat and sleep on the streets if you wish to chase her away."

An enormous dick sampler.

My face is showered with water from the hotel room shower, but it doesn't make me feel any better. Bryce shown that he is not someone to trifle with. Straightforward and concise. I'm not sure if I'm blessed or cursed. It's fortunate that he doesn't want a relationship. He's cursed for being a diversion.

I can't stop thinking about how he makes me feel. How I want to experience it over and over till I lose it all in a rush of ecstasy. Just thinking about it makes my heart race down there.

B*tch.

I quickly change into a fresh dress after my shower and make my way back down to the reception. Perhaps if I spend more time with other people, I won't worry about him as much.

There's music coming from the restaurant into the lobby. To provide for plenty of space for people to dance and socialize, the majority of the tables have been relocated and reconfigured.

It appears that every guest has been attended to. Many have already eaten and are dancing, enjoying the complimentary drinks, or doing both. Everyone is mixed together. This is just what the newlyweds wanted—cozy and pleasant.

There's a seat available for me, and the server seems to take my order like he would any other customer. Regardless of their affiliation with the hotel, he has been instructed to treat everyone like a guest even if I'm his boss.

I place an order for a glass of white wine, salmon, and a side salad. I'm ready to enjoy the remainder of the evening now that I'm not working.

In the center of the restaurant, the contented pair dances. James has relaxed for once, which is good. Before Tiffany came along, he was all about work and very much lived at the hotel. Despite my initial contempt for her, she has improved him. I never believed he would be able to achieve the level of equilibrium she offered him.

My food comes in an amazing amount of time. I let my shoulders drop and take a drink of my wine. Shade and Gabe walk into the restaurant right as I'm about to take my first bite.

After sensing the rhythm, Shade begins to walk in time, swaying her hips and spinning under Gabe's arm. He chooses to take a seat while she continues to do her thing, obviously not feeling the same beat as her.

She smoothly approaches Tiffany and James, giving them hugs and cheek kisses. She goes straight to the bar and places an order for a pink drink. Her gaze darts around the room before settling on me.

I lean my elbow on the table and cover my face with my hand, forming a face-shielding visor. It's Shade, but I attack my salad like a starving beast and hope she doesn't come over and say something wild. I ought to be more aware.

My prayers are ineffective. She immediately settles in at the table across from me.

"Mister?" Darkness descends.

I say, "Please don't," with my mouth full of food.

Her eyes roll. Did you honestly believe I would turn down the chance to congratulate you?

I swear, she is so dramatic. "I just don't feel like getting dragged right now."

She taunts, "You got more than dragged."

"Shadow."

"Denise."

"But her ex-boyfriend?" Shade chuckles. "I mean, of all the people, her ex included, who could have set it off?

aswell as at the lodging. at her nuptials. Even if I tried, I couldn't make this shit up.

Shade makes sensible judgments. Tiffany wasn't my favorite person before the wedding. Because of all the drama she brought to the hotel, I held her in high regard. I wasn't the biggest fan of Tiffany because of her antics with James at the hotel and her husband's antics when he came here. She seemed to me to be an opportunistic person searching for a way out. She seems to truly adore James, regardless of whether any of that is genuine. I no longer harbor resentment.

"Never fear. I reassure her that it was one and done. "I promise not to put myself in that predicament ever again."

"You know the one where you work and are hunched over a chair with your underwear pulled up?"

Before I can object, she stops me and says, "Girl, I'm just playing with you."

More worrying to me is that you're ignoring what appeared to be a nice dick in order to maintain your composure. It may be necessary for you to let that nigga run it back several times.

I assure her, "It was just a fleeting error in judgment."

"Girl, no one is condemning you." Did any of you manage to finish at all?

Bryce appears to be the star of a vivid dream as he enters the restaurant before I can answer her inquiry. reminding me of a planned yet unfulfilled delayed orgasm.

My mind is absorbed by the image of Bryce, and the room becomes blurry. I am unable to turn away. I feel as though there are volts coursing through my body and that the air is charged with electricity. The need to touch him, to run my hands down his jawline, to hold onto the back of his neck while he drives it home, makes my fingers twitch.

My gaze is met by Bryce, who gives me a mischievous smile. I make an effort to cool off, but my body fails me. Pussy just gave him a beating back.

It dawns on me then that Bryce is going to cause me problems. But I want to get into it for the first time in a long time.

As he approaches us, I pick up my wine and greedily take a big whiff from the remaining glass.

Shade examines my face intensely. "Are you okay over there?"

I make the error of glancing back Bryce's way. Shade looks at me, yelling as she turns back to face me.

She fanned me with her fingers and said, "He has you hot." "Look at you, wriggling and all."

"You are illogical," I attempt to brush her off.

"And you have to give that man the opportunity to take away your remaining senses."

"Girl," I grit my teeth and murmur as Bryce gets closer to the table.

How come? It was tidy. I could have expressed it simply. She touches her chin as if she's coming up with something clever. "Something like. "I was trying to be classy, but let that man lay that ass back and fuck the shit out of you." Bryce reaches the table just as she pushes back from it. She says, pretending to be innocent, "Hey, Bryce."

Before she can say anything more embarrassing to me, I say, "Bye, Shade."

Bryce nods respectfully and takes the seat that she just cleared. When a waiter arrives to take his order, he declines the assistance.

"You're not going to consume any food?" I inquire.

He looks directly into my eyes and says, "I want some cake," but I know he's not referring to the cake James and Tiffany will be slicing into shortly.

I can't even hold my breath when I think about him devouring my cake.

"Listen," I start, maintaining a steady tone. "Let's lay down some ground rules before you eat cake or anything else."

"I'm listening," Bryce adds, arching an eyebrow.

"Please, this is simply sex. I remind him that I have no interest in anything serious.

"I thought we had already discussed that part."

That was, however, prior to you casually approaching me and making fun of me once more.

"Me? Making fun of you? Bryce pushes his chair toward the table and takes a seat. "I believe you have it backwards. You first appear in the fitness center, staring at me like I'm a piece of meat.

"I saved you," I argue.

"After that, you sneak into my room to see my manhood," he says. At last, you drag me into a changing room without even completing the task at hand.

Although it's not exactly how it happened, I won't argue with you over untrue information. I simply want to make sure that we both understand one other. Just sex, I say, glancing at his face to gauge his response.

"Just sex," he says again.

"No residual emotions. Not a date. No feelings," I continue.

"None," he responds.

We look at each other for much longer than two people who have recently had sex should.

"Should we do this or something else?" After a long, awkward pause, Bryce finally breaks it.

Rather, it seems organic. cozy. Just two individuals assessing each other while they work toward a shared objective.

"Yes," I respond as I get up from the table and tip over my depleted wine glass. It breaks and catches other guests' attention.

Bryce is not going to let up, even though I start to kneel to clean up the mess.

"Oh no. He leads the way out and adds, "Come on."

I pretend not to care as we briskly pass every wedding guest. We're never quite reached by the elevators, and I'm starting to get restless.

It would only take a thought to push me over the edge—finally giving in to the very thing I've been denying myself for years. It feels like I'm walking a tightrope without a safety net, but the risk is exciting. Even though I know I'm playing with fire, I find it difficult to be concerned. Bryce is the one who can look after me tonight if anyone can.

The doors swing open. Calm and composed, we enter and wait for the doors to close. He pounces instantly. He goes in for a kiss. I lean my head back and give access to my neck, which he willingly accepts.

The feel of his lips on my collar bone sends shivers down my spine. He grabs the back of my neck, tearing into me without coming up for breath. His hand searches between my legs. Moaning when he feels the effect he has on me.

I

An enormous dick sampler.

My face is showered with water from the hotel room shower, but it doesn't make me feel any better. Bryce shown that he is not someone to trifle with. Straightforward and concise. I'm not sure if I'm blessed or cursed. It's fortunate that he doesn't want a relationship. He's cursed for being a diversion.

I can't stop thinking about how he makes me feel. How I want to experience it over and over till I lose it all in a rush of ecstasy. Just thinking about it makes my heart race down there.

B*tch.

I quickly change into a fresh dress after my shower and make my way back down to the reception. Perhaps if I spend more time with other people, I won't worry about him as much.

There's music coming from the restaurant into the lobby. To provide for plenty of space for people to dance and socialize, the majority of the tables have been relocated and reconfigured.

It appears that every guest has been attended to. Many have already eaten and are dancing, enjoying the complimentary drinks, or doing both. Everyone is mixed together. This is just what the newlyweds wanted—cozy and pleasant.

There's a seat available for me, and the server seems to take my order like he would any other customer. Regardless of their affiliation with the hotel, he has been instructed to treat everyone like a guest even if I'm his boss.

I place an order for a glass of white wine, salmon, and a side salad. I'm ready to enjoy the remainder of the evening now that I'm not working.

In the center of the restaurant, the contented pair dances. James has relaxed for once, which is good. Before

Tiffany came along, he was all about work and very much lived at the hotel. Despite my initial contempt for her, she has improved him. I never believed he would be able to achieve the level of equilibrium she offered him.

My food comes in an amazing amount of time. I let my shoulders drop and take a drink of my wine. Shade and Gabe walk into the restaurant right as I'm about to take my first bite.

After sensing the rhythm, Shade begins to walk in time, swaying her hips and spinning under Gabe's arm. He chooses to take a seat while she continues to do her thing, obviously not feeling the same beat as her.

She smoothly approaches Tiffany and James, giving them hugs and cheek kisses. She goes straight to the bar and places an order for a pink drink. Her gaze darts around the room before settling on me.

I lean my elbow on the table and cover my face with my hand, forming a face-shielding visor. It's Shade, but I attack my salad like a starving beast and hope she doesn't come over and say something wild. I ought to be more aware.

My prayers are ineffective. She immediately settles in at the table across from me.

"Mister?" Darkness descends.

I say, "Please don't," with my mouth full of food.

Her eyes roll. Did you honestly believe I would turn down the chance to congratulate you?

I swear, she is so dramatic. "I just don't feel like getting dragged right now."

She taunts, "You got more than dragged."

"Shadow."

"Denise."

"But her ex-boyfriend?"Shade chuckles. "I mean, of all the people, her ex included, who could have set it off? as well as at the lodging. at her nuptials. Even if I tried, I couldn't make this shit up.

Shade makes sensible judgments. Tiffany wasn't my favorite person before the wedding. Because of all the drama she brought to the hotel, I held her in high regard. I wasn't the biggest fan of Tiffany because of her antics with James at the hotel and her husband's antics when he came here. She seemed to me to be an opportunistic person searching for a way out. She seems to truly adore James, regardless of whether any of that is genuine. I no longer harbor resentment.

"Never fear. I reassure her that it was one and done. "I promise not to put myself in that predicament ever again."

"You know the one where you work and are hunched over a chair with your underwear pulled up?"

Before I can object, she stops me and says, "Girl, I'm just playing with you." More worrying to me is that you're ignoring what appeared to be a nice dick in order to maintain your composure. It may be necessary for you to let that nigga run it back several times.

I assure her, "It was just a fleeting error in judgment."

"Girl, no one is condemning you." Did any of you manage to finish at all?

Bryce appears to be the star of a vivid dream as he enters the restaurant before I can answer her inquiry. reminding me of a planned yet unfulfilled delayed orgasm.

My mind is absorbed by the image of Bryce, and the room becomes blurry. I am unable to turn away. I feel as though there are volts coursing through my body and that the air is charged with electricity. The need to touch him, to run my hands down his jawline, to hold onto the back of his neck while he drives it home, makes my fingers twitch.

My gaze is met by Bryce, who gives me a mischievous smile. I make an effort to cool off, but my body fails me. Pussy just gave him a beating back.

It dawns on me then that Bryce is going to cause me problems. But I want to get into it for the first time in a long time.

As he approaches us, I pick up my wine and greedily take a big whiff from the remaining glass.

Shade examines my face intensely. "Are you okay over there?"

I make the error of glancing back Bryce's way. Shade looks at me, yelling as she turns back to face me.

She fanned me with her fingers and said, "He has you hot." "Look at you, wriggling and all."

"You are illogical," I attempt to brush her off.

"And you have to give that man the opportunity to take away your remaining senses."

"Girl," I grit my teeth and murmur as Bryce gets closer to the table.

How come? It was tidy. I could have expressed it simply. She touches her chin as if she's coming up with something clever. "Something like. "I was trying to be classy, but let that man lay that ass back and fuck the shit out of you." Bryce reaches the table just as she pushes back from it. She says, pretending to be innocent, "Hey, Bryce."

Before she can say anything more embarrassing to me, I say, "Bye, Shade."

Bryce nods respectfully and takes the seat that she just cleared. When a waiter arrives to take his order, he declines the assistance.

"You're not going to consume any food?" I inquire.

He looks directly into my eyes and says, "I want some cake," but I know he's not referring to the cake James and Tiffany will be slicing into shortly.

I can't even hold my breath when I think about him devouring my cake.

"Listen," I start, maintaining a steady tone. "Let's lay down some ground rules before you eat cake or anything else."

"I'm listening," Bryce adds, arching an eyebrow.

"Please, this is simply sex. I remind him that I have no interest in anything serious.

"I thought we had already discussed that part."

That was, however, prior to you casually approaching me and making fun of me once more.

"Me? Making fun of you? Bryce pushes his chair toward the table and takes a seat. "I believe you have it backwards. You first appear in the fitness center, staring at me like I'm a piece of meat.

"I saved you," I argue.

"After that, you sneak into my room to see my manhood," he says. At last, you drag me into a changing room without even completing the task at hand.

Although it's not exactly how it happened, I won't argue with you over untrue information. I simply want to make sure that we both understand one other. Just sex, I say, glancing at his face to gauge his response.

"Just sex," he says again.

"No residual emotions. Not a date. No feelings," I continue.

"None," he responds.

We look at each other for much longer than two people who have recently had sex should.

"Should we do this or something else?" After a long, awkward pause, Bryce finally breaks it.

Rather, it seems organic. cozy. Just two individuals assessing each other while they work toward a shared objective.

"Yes," I respond as I get up from the table and tip over my depleted wine glass. It breaks and catches other guests' attention.

Bryce is not going to let up, even though I start to kneel to clean up the mess.

"Oh no. He leads the way out and adds, "Come on."

I pretend not to care as we briskly pass every wedding attendee. We're never quite reached by the elevators, and I'm starting to grow restless.

It would only take a thought to push me over the edge—finally giving in to the same thing I've been denying myself for years. It feels like I'm walking a tightrope without a safety net, yet the risk is exciting. Even though I know I'm playing with fire, I find it difficult to be concerned. Bryce is the one who can look after me tonight if anyone can.

The doors swing open. Calm and composed, we enter and wait for the doors to close. He jumps right in. He plants a kiss on her. I tilt my head back and allow him to feel my neck, and he takes it well.

I get chills just thinking about his lips on my collarbone. He seizes the nape of my neck and proceeds to rip into me, never pausing to catch his breath. His fingers straddle my legs. groaning when he perceives his impact on me.

HIS FOREHEAD AND PALMS ARE STARTING TO PERSPIRE, AND HIS EYES ARE TWITCHING. I CAN SEE IT EVEN THOUGH HE'S TRYING SO HARD TO DISGUISE IT. HE'S UNDER PRESSURE. IT'S BEEN AN EXHAUSTING HOUR. HE'S STARTING TO FEEL THE STRAIN; I'M GROWING.

"YOU SEE, MR. DUPREE, THERE'S NOT A SINGLE DIME I COULD SELL THAT PROPERTY FOR. ACCEPT IT OR REJECT IT. I RAISED MY VOICE.

ALTHOUGH I'VE HARDLY EVER DONE BUSINESS WITH A MULE LIKE THAT, I DO IT WHEN I MAKE THE DECISION TO TAKE A MAN FOR ALL OF HIS MONEY. NOBODY PROMISED THAT IT WOULD BE SIMPLE TO EXTRACT TWO MILLION DOLLARS FROM A CUNNING "LEGITIMATE" INVESTOR. HE WILL PURCHASE. BETTER FOR HIM TO BUY.

"I'M NOT BUYING," HE EXCLAIMS, GETTING TO HIS FEET AND MOTIONING FOR ONE OF HIS GUYS TO GET HIS HAT. "MR. GRAY, I APPRECIATE YOUR TIME, BUT I WAS HOPING FOR A BETTER OFFER. IT'S OBVIOUS THAT YOU STILL OWE YOUR OLD MAN A LOT.

YES, THAT IS NOT WHAT HE SAID.

I WAS HOPING TO BE ABLE TO REVEAL A SECRET CARD ON THE TABLE, BUT IT HAS COME TO THIS. "MR. DUPREE, I HEAR THAT YOU HAVE YOUR SIGHTS SET ON THE NIGHTCLUB ON THAT STREET FOR PURCHASE. WHAT BETTER TIME TO WHIP IT OUT?"

DUPREE STOPS, TURNS TO FACE ME. "WHAT ARE YOU TALKING ABOUT?" HE ASKS, TRYING TO LOOK UNINTERESTED. IT'S A TRADITIONAL PRANK. I WON'T BOTHER WITH THE DRAMA; HE'S EAGER TO LEARN HOW MUCH I KNOW.

"MR. DUPREE, YOU UNDERSTAND EXACTLY WHAT I'M TALKING ABOUT," I CONTINUE, TRACING MY FINGER OVER MY SHOT GLASS. YOU MIGHT FIND IT INTERESTING TO HEAR THAT I AM THE NEW OWNER. YOU HAVE BEEN

FRANTICALLY LOOKING FOR ME FOR THE PAST WEEK.

MEN LIKE DUPREE ARE STARTLED TO LEARN THAT I'VE ALWAYS BEEN ONE STEP AHEAD, AND THAT'S WHAT I LIVE FOR. LIKE A SATCHEL BEING EMPTIED, THE MAN COLLAPSES BACK ONTO THE CHAIR. "I DESIRE THAT STRUCTURE."

I SMILE AND SAY, "IT'S NOT FOR SALE."

"MR. GRAY, PLEASE!"

"NOT UNLESS YOU WISH TO GET TWO THINGS FOR THE PRICE OF ONE. IF YOU ACCEPT MY FIRST OFFER, I CAN SELL YOU BOTH OF THE PROPERTIES. INCLUDES A RESPECTABLE DISCOUNT.

DUPREE CHUCKLES. "DO YOU MEAN THAT I HAVE TO BUY BOTH OR NONE AT ALL?"

I SAY, "YOU PICK UP ON THINGS QUICKLY, MR. DUPREE," AND POUR

MYSELF ANOTHER ROUND OF WHISKEY TO TOAST TO YET ANOTHER SUCCESSFUL SALE AHEAD OF SCHEDULE.

MY PHONE RINGS RIGHT WHEN I FEEL LIKE THE DAY CAN'T GET ANY BETTER. THIS CALLER IS QUITE FASCINATING. SOMEONE WHO HAS FINALLY MADE UP HIS MIND, MUCH LIKE DUPREE.

CHAPTER 1: GET TO KNOW EMMA

EMMA CALLAHAN SPENT HER ENTIRE EARTHLY LIFE IN THE SMALL SEASIDE COMMUNITY OF SEABREEZE INLET. IT FELT LIKE HOME TO HER, WITH ITS COBBLESTONE STREETS, INTERESTING BISTROS, AND EXPANSIVE VIEWS OF THE OCEAN. EMMA WAS A WOMAN IN HER LATE TWENTIES, WITH HAZEL EYES THAT REFLECTED THE HUES OF THE SEA AND CHESTNUT HAIR THAT

CASCADED FREELY ABOUT HER SHOULDERS. SHE HAD GROWN UP IN A LOVELY, VERY OLD HOUSE THAT OVERLOOKED THE SEA; IT WAS A PLACE FULL OF TREASURED MEMORIES OF HER EARLY YEARS.

EMMA WAS DEEPLY ANXIOUS, EVEN IN SPITE OF THE PICTURESQUE SURROUNDINGS. HER LIFE HAD SETTLED INTO A PLEASANT ROUTINE THAT WAS NO LONGER FILLED WITH ASPIRATIONS AND DESIRES. SHE WAS A DEDICATED GRAPHIC DESIGNER WHO CHANNELED HER CREATIVITY INTO POSTERS FOR LOCAL BUSINESSES. SHE HAD A RELIABLE BOOKKEEPER NAMED IMPRINT, WITH WHOM SHE HAD A STEADY RELATIONSHIP FOR A WHILE. THOUGH THEIR COZY HOUSE HAD A WHITE PICKET WALL, EMMA COULDN'T HELP BUT WONDER

WHETHER THERE WAS MORE TO LIFE THAN THIS.

Mark was a good man who loved Emma with stability and dependability. Their love blossomed steadily and gradually after they met in school. He was the kind of person who usually remembered holidays and got her coffee bed on lazy Sunday mornings. Under the shining skies, he had proposed to her right here by the water, and she had said yes with determination.

But as the years went by, Emma was unable to shake the nagging feeling that something was missing. She was hungry for experience and vitality, the kind that uplifted and delighted. Mark had all the qualities Emma sought in an accomplice, but he lacked the sparkle.

One fateful night, Emma stayed by the sea, the cold sand between her toes, and thought about how her life had turned out as the sun set. She couldn't help but take advantage of the occasion to wonder if she would ever discover the drive and excitement she had secretly yearned for, or if she would always be forced to live a life of stability and comfort.

To her dismay, the rapid advances in technology were going to crash into her world, permanently altering her course and leading her to a love she had never imagined.

Chapter 4: The Emotional Storm

"The Tumult of Emotion," Chapter 4 of "The Journey of the First Kiss," captures the emotional roller coasters that Jane and David experience while they work through their sentiments. This chapter deftly examines self-discovery, emotional upheaval, and the difficulties of navigating adolescent relationships.

At the start of the chapter, David is still struggling to accept his unfulfilled love for Jane. His emotions are tumultuous; despite his best efforts to move on, every interaction with Jane triggers a wave of emotions he is attempting to repress. He immerses himself more in his books, turning to them as a means of escaping his surroundings. However, even when he is by himself, his mind frequently returns to Jane.

This chapter largely focuses on David's emotional journey. He begins recording his feelings and thoughts in a journal. His writings allow readers a more in-depth understanding of his mental terrain and encourage empathy for his struggles.

Jane, meantime, is also experiencing a whirlwind of emotions. Although she is dating Matt, she can't help but think about David. She's torn between her continued affections for David and her current connection with Matt. She misses her relationship with David, their easygoing exchanges, and their common goals.

Jane attempts to tell herself that she's happy with Matt in order to hide her feelings for David. Her heart, though, speaks a different language. She begins to doubt their connection as she experiences an unexplainable emptiness in spite of Matt's continuous presence.

This chapter's turning point occurs when Jane unintentionally comes across David's journal. She goes over his journal entries, his sincere declarations of love, his struggles with moving on, and his enduring feelings for her. Jane feels guilty and shocked by the realization. She understands how much she has wounded David and how much he loves her.

The story goes into more detail about Jane's inner turmoil after finding David's journal. Jane has a roller coaster of emotions as a result of David's raw feelings, including regret for accidentally hurting him, amazement at the depth of his feelings, and recognition of her unspoken love for him.

Jane struggles with these realizations and can't stop thinking back on their shared history and special bond. She begins to see how much she has undervalued David's influence in her life. She starts to realize how deeply she loves David, how much comfort he gives her, and how much he has been silently loving her all along.

David's path to recovery and acceptance is delicately depicted in the meantime. Despite the hurt it causes, he comes to terms with Jane's relationship with Matt over time. He values his friendship with Jane and does not want to part ways with her. He so chooses to keep up a friendly rapport with her while hiding his resentment behind a grin.

But when David finds out that Jane and Matt broke up, his mask comes off.

Hope rekindles in his heart despite his best efforts to keep it at bay. He can't figure out how Jane feels about him, so he's stuck in a loop of optimism and misery.

David and Jane have a moving exchange near the end of the chapter. Unintentionally, they end up meeting under their beloved old oak tree, where they enjoy a cozy moment of peace while watching the sun set. Their quiet communicates a great deal about their complicated relationship and their unspoken emotions. Their strong friendship and the unresolved emotions between them are highlighted in this intensely emotional scenario.

The chapter "The Tumult of Emotion" ends with Jane making a choice. She gives it a lot of thought before deciding to tell David how she really feels. She isn't sure how he will respond, but she knows she can't hide her emotions any longer.

I think Dean Andrews is dead!

I'm going to plan his death, even though I have no idea how. I'll also see to it that it aches.

Oh no. I want to let out a loud scream just by thinking about it. Perhaps very next to his ear, so that I might degrade his hearing the way he has degraded my life.

Not that I'm kidding.

Given that he destroyed my strategy, this is the least he deserves. Alright, so it's more of a serious intent than a strategy. a really serious intention.

Since, let's face it: I was holding out for the ideal first kiss. You know, the ideal location, the ideal moment, and the ideal boy. All the things a teenage girl who hasn't experienced her first kiss could ever hope for.

Not that I was eager to get to know it. All I could hope for was that it would occur soon. Perhaps even before I could earn my high school diploma.

Was that asking for too much? No, I didn't believe that.

However, it's possible that in a previous incarnation, I seriously angered Fate because she gave me the worst first kiss ever.

She could have planted a mediocre first kiss on me. However, she was forced to give me the worst. kiss first.

EVER THE WORST FIRST KISS

And now here I am, locked up in a cubicle in the girls' restroom, wishing with all my might that the last hour of my life had never happened. Alternatively, that time travel is possible and I could go back and reverse everything. In any case, I wish it had never happened.

"Finley"

"Are you here, Fin?"

My dearest buddies from fifth grade, Myles and Serena, have located me. I can no longer stay inside and wallow in my own misery.

I grudgingly yell, "In here." I groan and leave the cubicle, pushing off the closed toilet where I've been sitting.

Myles flinches at the sight of me. Are you alright?

Do I seem to be doing okay? My dark gray eyes are staring back at me as I raise my head to face the mirror.

You don't, that is true. You appear awful.

That's not even overstating the case. I typically presentable. I am rather proud of how I look. Even if I'm not the most stylish girl in the class, I'll never be found appearing disheveled.

To correct: would never be apprehended.

My dark auburn hair, which I spent fifteen minutes perfectly curling this morning, has the appearance of a bird's nest. It is armpit length. And the adorable pink dress I got from a resale shop a few months ago is totally ruined by stains from fruit juice.

All because I foolishly happened to pass by when that moron was having fun with his pals. Even how it happened eludes me. Before I knew it, his lips were on mine.

I got kissed by him!

And he had the audacity to appear as astonished as I did when I shoved him off me.

Naturally, I had to take action. I hurled the contents of my canned strawberry juice at him because he had just embarrassed me in front of the entire cafeteria, and I was still traumatized by their collective scream. And I stumbled on the liquid and fell to the floor when I tried to storm off.

I've been repeating it over and over in my thoughts ever since it happened.

I'm going to kill Dean Andrews, for real, I swear!

This is where. Serena pulls me out of my agony and says, "Change into this. This is a knitted green dress that looks like it belongs in the seventies, but it's definitely not one of those adorable vintage looks I always see on Pinterest." Not at all.

I look at it horrified. "Where did you discover that object? "Lost and Found"

Indeed. That was the only respectable one I could locate within that. Apologies.

I hurriedly put on the hideous dress after taking off my gorgeous one, letting out a dejected breath. "Aww. Even the smell is mothball-like.

Serena flinches. That is awful. However, it's not as though you have another outfit.

"I understand," I murmur. "This really isn't my day."

Myles points out to us, "And it's about to get worse." She's staring at her phone. "TikTok already has it."

How?

Serena exclaims, "No way," her pale blue eyes enlarging with fear. She rushes to Myles and takes a quick look at the screen. I can see the affirmation clearly written on her face when she turns to face me again.

I tightly close my eyes. There must be a dream here. A nightmare come true. Not at all, a nightmare. This is the worst nightmare ever!

"It's amazing that they captured the entire event on camera. With her long platinum blonde hair flipped over her shoulder, Serena steps in front of the mirror and complains, "They didn't even consider your feelings."

"What were your expectations? Myles laughs, "These people are savages," and tucks her phone back into her purse, blocking me from seeing the video. which indicates to me how awful it looks.

"How can I get out of this?" I stutter in fear.

You'll manage to solve it. She stands next to Serena and strokes her light brown hair, which has just been cut into a stylish bob. "You always do," she says.

Serena looks up at me. Fin, don't worry about it. In a week or two, I'm sure they'll forget about it.

"Two weeks or one week?" I weep.

She smiles pitifully at me. "A couple of days?"

I let out a loud groan and rest my hip on the vanity counter. "No, you're entirely correct. And that would be overly optimistic.

If I'm lucky, the junior class at Alcott High will discuss it for an entire month. similar to the Missy Summers event from the previous year. The poor kid feared she had pooped her pants when she inadvertently sat on a chocolate bar. She sobbed in the nurse's office for the remainder of the day, and for the next few weeks, she growled at anyone who tried to bring up the incident. She also went on a blocking binge on Instagram and TikTok, as I recall.

I really don't want to place myself in that circumstance. The blocking part is fine with me, but the snarling part? Not at all. Not in a manner. That seems really demanding.

Thus, I'd prefer to just not deal.

Alternatively, you could just kick Dean in the butt and have Myles or Serena capture the entire event. Everyone would have something more engaging to discuss as a result.Alternatively, it might backfire catastrophically," I mumble to myself.

"What is that?" Serena pokes at it.

"I'm planning to kill Dean."

"That sounds like fun." Myles smiles. "Need our assistance?"

"When I have a good plan, I'll let you know," I say. "I believe I'll return home and call it a day. I'm going to the nurse's office to try to get a permission slip. I don't even need to act like I'm experiencing a headache. One is already starting to feel brewing.

I pick up my damaged garment with a scowl. I'm sure it will be difficult for me to remove the stains.

Oh, I'm going to love butting his ass.

The remainder of the day flew by. Not because Nick kept kissing me, but rather because I kept seeing the kisses in my head. Thoughts of why the hell he did that would occasionally cross my head, but I would immediately discard them in order to maintain my happy zone.

I sneaked looks at him whenever I got the chance. His eyes frequently showed the same agony they had that morning when he had allowed me in the door. But when he saw me glancing at him, it would vanish into a radiant smile.

He had a thought about something. Even though it should have mattered, I wasn't sure what it was or whether it even mattered. I just enjoyed the fact that I could have made him grin at the moment when he was clearly confused about anything.

I was hoping for an invitation to lunch at the end of our shift, but I never received one. It was difficult to concentrate about anything else after the way he kissed me today, but the unpredictable nature became annoying.

After leading me outside to my truck, Nick positioned me between the open door and the cab. His other hand made its way to my hip while his right one remained on the top of the truck. "I have a lot to get done today, so I'd ask that you remain and eat lunch. "How about tomorrow?" he murmured, drawing me in until our hips were in contact.

I sucked in the corner of my lower lip, thrilled with happiness. "Yeah, that sounds good," I muttered.

His lips turned up at the edges and he started to twinkle. Then today, without saying anything, he knelt down and claimed my lips once more. He began slowly, brushing his lips across my. His tongue brushed my lower lip, pleading for permission to enter. And once inside, he viciously attacked my mouth. I adored it.

I moistened my lips, wanting to taste every last morsel of him when he withdrew. It caused him to chuckle and smile. And then, for no apparent reason, my jaw dropped open and I shouted something incredibly dumb.

"Whatever became of the whole trying to stop petting and kissing me thing?" With a laugh of my own, I questioned, and then winced when my mind realized what I had really uttered.

Nick gave me a stern look and then a small smile appeared on his lips. He answered, "That was me trying." He pressed his lips to my ear, sealing what little space remained between us. "Can you imagine the situation if I hadn't made the attempt?"

The thought of it made me gasp. If this was how he was setting himself aside, it would have been scorching hot. He gave me a gentle peck on the lips and turned to go as the intensity of the thought subsided.

As I drove home, all kinds of ideas ran through my head. It was difficult to accept that I had really urged him to quit doing whatever it was we were doing, and he had truly promised to try. He tried to give me a stupid kiss for a split second, haha.

After 45 minutes, I arrived in the driveway. I changed into my farm clothes immediately and went to visit the alpacas. I was contacted first by Nick. I knew he was in for a wonderful treat. I was reminded of Nick gripping my hips right before bringing me in for a kiss when he nudged my hip.

Grinning, I pulled out a goodie for him. Like the genuine Nick always did, he accepted it politely and trotted off. I scowled at the idea. Whenever I felt like leaving him, he would yank me back in, practically putting his large, powerful hands on my hips.

I whispered, willing the thoughts of him to go, "Stop it."

Coming up behind me, my dad exclaimed, "Stop what, honey?"

The sound of his voice made me jump. Oh, not at all. A butthead was acting out among the alpacas.

He shot me a wry smile. "Don't you think they're cute?"

I gave a nod.

"I value the investigation you conducted. I had hoped that this spring's initial shaving would have been better, but I was unaware that the person who sold them to me had shaved them right before to collect as much fur as possible. His frown replaced his smile. "Throughout the winter, the poor things hardly had any insulation."

It was depressing. The proprietor, from whom my dad had purchased them, pilfered the animals' winter coats in order to profit a little more. Fortunately, the winter had been mild and they had a barn big enough to allow them to stay inside. Living in Colorado, you never know when the weather will be harsh or pleasant at times. The majority of the time, they were inside. They performed flawlessly. We missed out on a spring cutting, but we'll make up for it next year because we waited so long," I informed him with hope.

He scratched his neck and whispered, "I hope you're right, honey." "How's work going, then?"

I gave a shoulder shrug. "It's alright, Dad," I answered.

He said, "There's a boy you like," more like a statement than a query.

I was taken aback by it and my eyes expanded. I said, "How did you know?"

My father chuckled. "There was Nick, followed by Frosty, Blanco, Chocolate, Twinkle toes, and a host of other strange names. Honey, it wasn't difficult to figure out.

I wanted to hide as my cheeks went cherry red. I had never discussed males with my parents. Never had cause to do so. And that was just as uncomfortable as I had anticipated.

He gave me a shoulder pat and turned as like he was about to leave. He added, "I promised your mother I wouldn't lecture you," though, before continuing. However, because you'll soon be eighteen, please take precautions. Then he vanished.

I inhaled deeply and suppressed a cry. I knew all about defending myself in sexual situations, but because my heart had already been broken, I wished someone had taught me how to guard it instead.

I contacted Marlow after finishing my daily chores and giving the other alpacas a reward. Although she had already heard, I had hoped to speak with her before she learned what had transpired with Craig.

"Really, Aurora?" she remarked mockingly. "Nick is an asshole with two timing. You let him handle you like a puppet because he has a fucking girlfriend. It's difficult to watch, damn it! And then you use a kind guy to ruin something wonderful.

He took some actual shots in the stomach; he nearly sobbed; and he lay motionless on the floor for some time. "I should have known; I should have watched them," he thought to himself. It had seemed odd, thinking back, that no one had come seeking for him, but he had to get home now. With an utter determination, he moved onto his hands and knees and immediately forced his body up so he could examine the damage. It did not hurt him as much as he had anticipated. It stung inside, not in his gut. He knew a black eye was coming as he saw himself in the mirror, but the redness above his left eye indicated that they missed more than they connected. Pushing out and walking home, he turned away from the classroom and headed out the bathroom door. His stomach began to hurt as he moved, causing him to sag forward and walk with a noticeable stooped posture. When they got home, he told them what had transpired. After assessing the damage, Mom put him to bed. ""We'll wait for your dad to return home." She talked about it like it was a small altercation.

When Whitey's father got there, he was fast asleep. He checked the youngster over after waking him. "We will talk tomorrow," he stated. Whitey turned over, but he did not close his eyes. "Let me consider the appropriate response to this," was what his father intended to say. Whitey got up before dinner, trying to forget about the extraordinary evening that was in store. Whitey didn't express it, but he believed his parents saw this as a necessary part of maturing and learning how to coexist. They allowed him to resolve his issues on his own terms, knowing that he did not have the same standing as his classmates. He had to rely on God to guide him along the route that God would choose for him in life.

The youngster was awake when his father came the following day; his mother had kept him from school. He had a sore middle area and had trouble seeing out of his left eye, along with a knot just above the black eye. They did not discuss the incident or the beatings while they were having dinner. Dad suggested that they have a conversation while sitting on the back porch while Mom cleaned up the kitchen, which was often the boy's allotted duty.

"You know if you do not do something, you will have to put up with this for the remainder of the school year, and possibly for the duration that you live here," he said at the beginning. There will always be those boys. You would still have to deal with them even if you went to the principal. I've heard they have no fear of anyone.

"What actions should I take?"

You really need an equalizer, son. Additionally, you must comprehend what a bully is, and those five are exactly that. Together, they exude fearlessness. The stronger leader is the source of their power. They lack bravery when left alone; even the most powerful person derives their strength from those who follow them. Something to give you the advantage, this. Come in later tomorrow, perhaps around midday when everyone is outside. Take advantage of this, approach the largest one, and strike him repeatedly with it. If he follows you, flee and don't allow him to hit you once more. The bully will back down if you fight back; they will move on to a less vulnerable target if they perceive that you will not back down. He gave Whitey a wool sock, and a very big sweet potato was inside. Use it like a club, he clarified. You'll have the upper hand and they'll stop bothering you once they see you're not afraid to fight back.

Whitey did what his father said and took the sock and swung it around.

Whitey hit the railing, which was covered with a raincoat. After it burst, he declared, "All right, I'm ready." I'm returning to school tomorrow.

The dating scene is changing so quickly that many people are puzzled and bewildered. Every day, hundreds of fresh possible dates arrive in your inbox from online dating services. With phone apps, hooking up is as simple as ordering takeout. We've become a generation of serial daters, seeking quick sexual fulfillment through one-night stands and casual sex, thanks to the "hook-up" culture. Many people feel hollow when physical pleasure is prioritized over forming bonds with others. They are unable to identify what it is that they are missing. They are passing on the million sexy things to do between the first kiss and sex because they are in a hurry.

The majority of us have accepted that "instant access" is a part of every aspect of our everyday existence. We've grown accustomed to expecting things like a prompt reply to our texts, same-day delivery of our online orders, and weight loss of 10 pounds in three days.

The myth that obtaining our desires as quickly as possible leads to happiness is harming our bodies, souls, and sexual lives. Quick satisfaction is similar to a narcotic that makes you feel happy for a short while before making you realize that you're left with a hole that might never be filled. Even if you are sharing your most private self with several people, the addiction feeds the drive to never stop searching for the next fix and leaves you feeling hopeless and alone.

We may have perfected the quick and simple thrill, but we've forgotten the subtle art of seduction. Have we turned into our own worst enemies in our race to get to the point of wanting sex? Are we putting our future at serious risk because of our insatiable need for the now?

It is not intended for A Million Things to take months to implement. It's not a justification to put off someone you're not truly attracted to. This book is intended for those who are genuinely interested in developing their relationship and making it work such that great desire is attained and maintained throughout time. These are the kind of folks who would gladly give up instant gratification for the exquisite practice of relishing passion as it naturally develops.

A plethora of books and material are accessible regarding relationships and the development of intimacy, trust, and connection. Although these subjects will be covered to some extent, I want to concentrate on the area that is rarely mentioned because of rejection, shame, or even fear. This book provides a detailed road map for building desire, arousal, trust, and intimacy in a sensuous and gentle way. It is created for couples whose relationship has become stale over time as well as for individuals who are really interested in finding a matching partner, boyfriend, girlfriend, or future marriage. The commitment to pursuing a close, passionate, and emotional connection that has the greatest possibility of igniting intense desire throughout the relationship will be advantageous to everyone who is interested in doing so.

This is a novel approach to get a better understanding of your partner's desire, fantasies, inhibitions, and sexual expertise before engaging in full-blown sex. This procedure may take longer if you or your spouse are timid or introverted, but it is even more crucial that you take your time. Only go to the next level when you are completely at ease with each step. In today's culture, it is common to have sex before any meaningful closeness is developed. While many individuals find this to be temporarily satisfying, this may be because they haven't looked into alternative paths to deep and permanent connection.

Maybe it's time to revive the forgotten art of making out and rediscover the magnificent power of the "slow reveal." The objective is to slowly develop sexual tension and explore each other until you are genuinely "on fire with desire." You will be left wondering about twisted sheets and the tangible heat of bodies entwined in passionate acrobatics—it's actually a mental and physical dance.

We reach great peaks of sensation and need when something that is typically offered too quickly in our society is postponed and temporarily unattainable. These days, it happens so infrequently that your brain, trained to get everything instantly, finds it hard to comprehend what ought to be a normal delay. This instills in you a sense of perceived worth and longing for the person you are waiting for.

A fine dining experience doesn't happen in ten minutes. It is served to you one delectable dish at a time so you can savor each taste and appreciate each course. A dinner like this is prepared and served so that every taste is completely enjoyed, both as an individual element and in its distinctive pairings. When the experience is planned properly, there are opportunities to stop and pique interest in the upcoming course. There is no doubt that you will feel full after eating this dinner. Similarly, we will apply strategies that increase anticipation and fulfillment in our relationships. There will be a ton of incredible surprises in store for you if you come along on this adventure with me as you establish the mind, brain, and body connection.

Roderick's thoughts about that evening persisted till the burial. He found it unbearable to simply look at his infant. It hurt too much. All he wanted was to hold his lovely wife once more. How was he going to raise a kid by himself? And yet a girl! Without Jane's direction, how could he be a good father?

***

It had been seven years since Ann's mother passed away that evening. Ann had developed into a daring little child who bore a striking resemblance to her mother. Same smile, same glint in her eyes, same silky brown hair. She did not, however, behave in any way like Roderick remembered Jane. Ann refused to be tamed, despite Roderick's repeated warnings to her to cease acting foolishly. Jane was always very nice, gentle, and ladylike.

Roderick experienced a stirring in his emotions each time he saw his daughter's reflection of his wife; it was almost as though Jane's spirit was reaching out to him, attempting to instill a sense of love and tranquility. However, Roderick pushed aside any sentiments of consolation when this occurred. He would lose himself in his task the moment he felt at ease.

Ann used to play tricks and taunt Neala, the housemaid, all the time. She would also rush down the hallways and slide down the stairs. Because Ann couldn't pronounce Neala when she was younger, she began referring to her as Nana. Neala raised Ann as if she were her own kid, even though her job description only called for her to be the housemaid. As Ann grew older and more rowdy, Neala found herself yelling more and more after her. "Ann, halt! Your dad would be really angry! However, Neala knew that Ann was pleased, and both of them realized that she didn't really mind.

Ann played by herself in the mornings most days. When she became bored, she would follow Neala around, occasionally lending a hand but usually causing trouble while she cleaned. Ann would abandon her current task around midmorning and quickly head to the stables, where Henry would be completing his morning duties. Despite Ann being two years older than Henry, they remained the closest of friends. Every morning, Henry would assist his father George Stewart, who worked in the stable house for Mr.Blockstone, in feeding the horses and maintaining the facilities. It was Henry's intention to acquire these abilities in order to become a stableman himself eventually.

Ann occasionally watched Henry while he worked with his father. She wanted to assist with feeding and brushing the horses, but she couldn't enter the stables because it was too risky for a small child. She would pace in front of the stable entrance rather than enter. George would smile to himself as he watched Ann eagerly waiting for Henry. He would even obnoxiously inform Henry that he might not be able to go play because of how much work there was. Next, he would cast a sidelong glance toward Ann, who would have froze at the sound of this. Ann would stomp her tiny foot on the ground and put her hands on her hips to express her outrage at Mr. Stewart's joke, while George would laugh and send Henry outside to play. However, Ann and Henry left the area quickly, acting as though the sun would set in a matter of minutes, so their outrage didn't last long.

Henry and Ann used to go on excursions together every time they were together. They would sometimes creep into the woods and pretend to be monkeys climbing trees, or they would pretend to be pirates searching for hidden riches by going down to the river. Neala would also always tell Ann to change out of her clothes and wash her face right away before her father arrived home. Neala was reluctant to let Ann play outside too much for fear of upsetting Mr.Blockstone once more.

But Roderick would constantly observe that Ann always ended up with scratches and scrapes. He would scream at Neala for letting Ann play outside once more. "Neala, you're giving the girl too much freedom!"

Additionally, he disapproved of the stable boy's influence on his daughter and consistently urged Ann to stay inside and do crafts like sewing and drawing. He got her some pencils and drawing paper. "Ann, draw me a picture," he would say. "Do you have any embroidery skills?"

Brenn didn't even realize he had fallen asleep when he woke up abruptly. Joey was no longer in the bed, and she was no longer in his arms.

Joey!

"This is where I am."

Brenn followed Joey's voice into the living room, where he was seated in the big leather recliner and enjoying the view from the window.

"What is the duration of your awake?"

Joey gave him a quick look. Merely a few minutes. It looks like you awoke immediately after me.

"You alarmed me," Please don't do that again.

"Don't be alarmed, or don't you get out of bed and let that bulldozer snore all over again?"

"Little cheeky shit." After shooing Joey over, he discovered they couldn't fit on the chair side by side and took Joey onto his lap. He gave him a tight hug and instinctively nuzzled the nape of his neck. He bit Joey's shoulder and said, "When I go to sleep with a man in my arms, I expect him to be there when I wake up."

"You don't do that very often? drift off to sleep holding a man in your arms?

"No, I usually tell them to bugger off after I fuck them."

"Yuck, nasty."

Brenn smiled. I've never really slept through the night with a man. I slept with them all night, although...

Joey gave him a painful shove. "Stop talking about fuckings now. I will get envious of you.

Feeling envious? B*tch.Brenn hoped. He gestured toward the glass through which Joey had been gazing. "What were you examining?"

"The shoreline."

Yes? Do you enjoy being at the beach?

"I used to be a surf lifeguard."

Brenn was shocked by the confession. He hadn't thought about what Joey had done prior to getting sick. "Where? In Sydney, huh?

"Kiama."

Brenn said, "That down there is beautiful." Kiama, a gorgeous spot overlooking the Pacific Ocean on the south coast, was just a few hours away.

That's my residence there. lived. Joey looked away from the window. "The beach, the sea, and the sun are some of the things I'm going to miss." Brenn had never seen such bleakness in his eyes, and his tone was melancholy.

"Would you like to return?"

"To Kiama?" Joey gave a shrug. "There's nothing down there for me anymore, but I wouldn't mind going one last time." I sold my house and donated the proceeds to the lifeguard fund because my grandma passed away shortly before I realized I was ill.

"That's very kind of you."

"As if I were taking it with me." Joey's eyes gleamed with humor once more. "I could have, however, chosen to go in style like an Egyptian king and have gold lining my coffin."

Brenn joked, knowing he would either have to ride the joke with Joey or suffer in silence. "I don't think the pallbearers would have been able to lift it," Brenn said.

Joey smiled and pulled herself up into Brenn's chest. He hummed in delight and remarked, "You're nice and warm."

Brenn gave Joey's naked back a gentle massage. "I'm only warm because of how cold you are. You ought to have dressed more elegantly than these skimpy, if quite attractive, black boxers.

Joey whispered, pointing out the obvious: "You're naked."

Indeed, but I am roughly a hundred pounds heavier than you.

"But you're not fat."

"No, you're not fat."

Joey recoiled and gave him a pained expression. "Hey, you mentioned how gorgeous my body was."

"Yes, but you should put on more weight."

"What's the purpose?"

With a smile on his face, Brenn caressed Joey's thigh, enjoying the feel of his flesh and, more importantly, the fact that he could settle Joey's disagreements regarding food. Your vitality is depleted each time you experience an orgasm. You won't have enough to orgasm once again if you don't refill it. Joey, don't you want to come?

Joey rolled his eyes, seemingly satisfied with that response.

"So, you must increase your energy levels."

Through eating, Joey complained.

Indeed, but that won't cause you any trouble. I offered you a drink that was as energetic as an orgasm."

Brenn concluded that Joey didn't need to know even though there was more.

Just one? So I have to drink more if I want more?"

I always assumed you were intelligent.

"Did I tell you about the part about not playing fairly?" Joey muttered once more.

Brenn grinned and cited, "In love and war, everything is fair."

Joey countered, "We're not at war," but from the expression in his eyes, he could tell what Brenn would say next.

"No, that's fair; I'm in love with you."

Joey let out a moan. It would have been preferable for me to remain in the hospital. If I said no, at least people accepted it there.

"I should have considered that before bringing you home with me." Brenn smiled, understanding that Joey's flimsy objections were really an act of ungracious surrender. Brenn liked it better than Joey just complying with all of his requests.

Brenn felt a warm kiss above his right nipple a few seconds after Joey snuggled back into his chest. "What are you doing?" he inquired, taken aback that such a small action could cause his body to tense and his heart to race.

"Starving to get hungry." Brenn felt a warm thrill up his spine at Joey's soft giggle. Not that Brenn wasn't halfway there just by having Joey in his arms, but Joey's next kiss got him hard.

As Joey dragged her warm tongue across his nipple, he said, surprised. "Do you know what you're doing?"

"I'm starving to death." After shifting in Brenn's arms, Joey focused on Brenn's other nipple. "Are you also becoming hungry?" With a serious tone, Joey inquired.

Brenn's back arched and he groaned. Joey's touch on him was too exquisite for him to resist. "Yes."

Joey fell to the floor politely at Brenn's confession and then pushed his thighs apart. Joey knelt between Brenn's legs and grasped his cock in his hands, but Brenn didn't stop him since he could see the resolve in Joey's eyes. The mouth that devoured him was warm and willing, even though the delicate touch was lovely. Brenn was concerned that Joey might choke because Joey took so much into his throat this time instead of just surrounding the tip. Brenn made a swift attempt to retreat. Joey stopped him with her sharp teeth.

Joey, please don't.

Joey relaxed. Desire to. Like it," he murmured before collapsing once more.

Brenn had seen more than his fair share of blowjobs; some were skillful, some clumsy, but this one was unmatched. Joey took him all the way down to the root, and then, with strong muscles in his throat, swallowed him whole.

Joey, screw you!

After pulling up, Joey inhaled deeply, smiled, and embraced him once more. Brenn moaned as he felt his eyes drift to the back of his head. If Joey did it again, he was pretty sure he would come, but Joey pulled off him and gasped.

7 - View of the Garden

TJ went to ring the bell at the front desk.

The attractive woman said, "May I help you?"

"Please give me a room for tonight and tomorrow. What do you have that faces south? I enjoy the sun in the morning.

"All right, honey. That works out to $8 each night plus $4 for the key deposit. That amounts to $20. When you turn in the key, you'll get your $4 back. Over there, coffee is available around-the-clock, and breakfast is served from six to nine in the morning. Honey, I have a great room upstairs. Although it's not a garden, you'll get plenty of sunlight.

"What time does the pool open?"

Oh, my dear, it's closed for the season already. Next door, the Waffle House is open. There are also twenty-four hours. All the way down to room number 236 upstairs, then, my dear.

TJ produced ten dollar bills and ten one-cent bills. She turned, picked up the key, thanked him, and left.

"Would you like a receipt?"

"Oh, I'm sorry, no thanks." TJ located the steps and descended all the way to the top. The place was tastefully simple inside. There was a nightstand with a lamp and a queen-size bed. There were two windows in the corner that faced southwest. A tiny table and two seats were located in the area beneath the windows. It appears as though the room was equipped from home. It was a bureau instead of a closet. There was a little vase filled with fresh flowers on the table beneath the window. To unpack her backpack, TJ opened the bureau. Her outfit needed to be ironed because the journey had left its mark. Just to hear the noise, she turned on the television. It was Merv Griffin's show. She was not a big fan of talk shows. This was when she was normally in school. She was aware that Rick wouldn't get home from work for a short while. She had no idea how he would respond to the knowledge that she had fled. She merely wanted to go to the dance; it's not like she was intending to stay away.

TJ determined it would be best for her to remain in the hotel and avoid going too far. She would wait for Rick's work to end before calling him. She spent some time watching TV before it became monotonous. She went to write in her diary while sitting near the window. As it was getting close to six o'clock, she became hungry. She strolled toward the Waffle House in order to get dinner. She noticed a man staring at her from inside his car as she was strolling through the parking lot.

She called him a creep as she passed.

TJ settled down at the bar. She perused the menu. She had to order something filling and inexpensive.

"Hello Hon, what may I get you?"

"Waffle, sunny-side up egg, and sweet tea."

"Getting up."

TJ read the "Odessa American" while she waited, taking a portion of it with her. She ate slowly. She wanted to allow Rick some time for cleaning up and eating. When the waitress arrived, she placed the check down. She took out a couple of bucks and placed them down. She took a dime and left the rest when she delivered the change.

"Please give me some more tea. I'm grateful.

She approached the phone and dialed Rick's number. After giving him a brief overview of her travels, she invited him to stop over and spend a short while. He said he will be there in thirty minutes, and he was thrilled to hear from her. Returning, she read the remainder of the paper and drank more tea. She made the decision to go clean up because she was full of waffle.

TJ made his way to the motel from the Waffle House. She paused at the outer boundary of the parking area and collected a pair of untamed Honey Daisies. She picked a few to give to Rick to take home and tucked one into her hair. She turned to stroll back up the stairs, picking daisy peddles.

Rva arrives at Cafe Barcelona ahead of schedule and waits outside for Ethan. This cafe is located at the further end of town, and she has never been there. Within the football community, it's a well-liked cafe. She's not sure why. I'll find out today. She paces nervously in her pencil heels while thinking. I don't need to win Ethan over. Then why did Ana urge me to put on these heels? My toes, oh! Eva looks around for Ethan as she flexes her toes and casually moves her palm across her knee-length skater dress in royal blue.

Ethan enters. Eva gapes at the sight of Ethan strolling down the other street, body hugging a gray tee and blue pants. His hands are tucked into his pockets as he strolls, flaunting his flawless, powerful, and toned arms. He gives Eva a soft wave, but she responds with a vigorous shout. He bear-hugs Eva as he crosses the street.

"Hello, Eva!" Says Ethan. "It looks great on you, girl."

Hello, Ethan. Eva exclaims with joy. Ethan's good looks have her completely enamored. With his brilliantly carved face, dimpled cheekbones, blue eyes, and amazing physique, he resembles the Greek God. Eva had never seen a more attractive man than him; he is incredibly handsome. Eva is happy to have some alone time with him at last. Otherwise, the football players are all around him.

They enter the cafe. Eva isn't shocked to discover flags from several football-mad nations hanging on the walls, LED displays all over the place playing World Cup highlights, and a house full of people drinking beer while transfixed to the TVs.

"Hi Jake." Jake gets a knuckle bump from Ethan.

"This place is managed by Jake." Eva is introduced to Jake by Ethan.

"Hello, Jake." says Eva.

Jake offers them a seat at the table with a smile. Ethan pauses to watch the LED screen match.

"Oh my god! He ought to have handed it to Ronaldo after dribbling it. Ethan says something. "Incorrect action. Beck is there to take over, and it's so clear that the idiot doesn't let him pass. Barca desires total dominance. Ethan runs a hand through his gelled blond hair while he tweets about the footwork.

"Ethan." Eva phones Ethan, who is deeply engaged in the game.

Eva walks over to the table that Jake has indicated. She watches Ethan witness the match for a bit before giving up. He just wants to play because he is such a youngster. She enjoys seeing him pose, showcasing his toned abs, while keeping his eyes glued to the screen. "May I kiss him right now?" "You cannot, I assure you. Hold on to the very end. Ana's voice plays in her head while she speaks to herself.

Is he the right guy? How will being with him feel?

"You will always be his second priority. He's thinking about football and always will.

Eva begins to experience all of the negative ideas.

Why is he addicted to the screen if you are out on a date? Just give it some thought.

"I apologize to Eva for keeping you waiting." Ethan interrupts Eva's thought process by sitting in the chair.

"No issue." Eva grinned. "It must be a crucial game that we shouldn't miss."

"No, I have seen that match a lot of times. However, it grabs my attention each time I see it. A small smile spreads across Ethan's left cheek as he speaks.

The waiter arrives and offers them salads and protein shakes.

"I hope it's okay with you. I can only have this, you know. Thus, I placed the same order for you.

Eva glances at the protein shake and the boring-looking carrot-lettuce salad. She manages to say, "No problem," and chews her bottom lip.

"My life's love is football." Says Ethan, "Gorging the salad."

Eva looks at him as she uses her fork to take up a bite. She is swallowing the bland salad as he stuffs it like a cow.

"Is this something you want?" Ethan takes out a tiny vial from his pocket and holds it up. Eva scowls. "Seeds of Chia" Says Ethan.

"Thanks, but no."

Ethan adds a dash of it to his protein smoothie. Eva considers what to do with the beverage. Having dinner at home early and coming here later would have been preferable. I could have saved myself the trouble of having to eat this that way. Gulping down the protein shake.

Ethan talks about his aspirations for his football career, saying that he wants to join the club team, go from there, and make millions of dollars. Then, at such a young age, he talks about his accomplishments, his squad, and his newest possession—the brand-new, ostentatious black BMW. Hearing everything about Ethan bores Eva. If this is how it's going to be with him, my man? Instead of a football game, I need a love life.

After finishing his meal, Ethan glances at Eva's plate.

"You haven't had any food. Are you alright? Ethan queries.

Eva wants to convince him that she is a completely normal girl and that he is the weird one who goes on dates with salads and protein shakes. She doesn't tell him, though.

"I have too much food." I ate dinner early. Eva lies to herself, grinning. Should I even give this frog a kiss? She ponders.

"Eating dinner early is healthy. You worry too much about your diet. That's nice. Eva fakes a grin while Ethan compliments her, and Eva mentally curses Ethan.

Shall we now depart? I'd like not to have any more. Eva responds, her eyes gleaming with fun and her smile staying intact inside.

Alright. Where would you like to go? My position? Today, we get access to the FIFA match highlights. You can cheer them on while I observe. Ethan suggests that they watch TV in his house. Sounds pitiful, Ethan. She ponders.

www.ingramcontent.com/pod-product-compliance
Lightning Source LLC
Chambersburg PA
CBHW052150110526
44591CB00012B/1931